For my mother and father,
Susan and Don Cundieff,
who gave me this life.

DARLING NOVA

WINNER OF THE 2017 AUTUMN HOUSE POETRY PRIZE

DARLING NOVA

MELISSA CUNDIEFF

Autumn House Press
Pittsburgh

Autumn House Press receives state arts funding support through a grant from the Pennsylvania Council on the Arts, a state agency funded by the Commonwealth of Pennsylvania, and the National Endowment for the Arts, a federal agency.

Cover art: "Lost Communication" by Naomi Vona. Collage. 3.9 x 5.7 inches.
Book & cover design: Joel W. Coggins

ISBN: 978-1-938769-30-6
Library of Congress Control Number: 2017958572

CONTENTS

And at the back of what we've done
There is the knowledge of you.

—Joanna Newsom

DARLING NOVA

WHO NOW TO REBEL AGAINST

I have a cigarette to smoke and a map
of the city where I was born. Four hours
from here, my two kids fly a kite before dinner.

I'm driving away from a childhood
friend's funeral. She died badly, her mother
embarrassed and hiding the cause which, turns out,

was hepatitis exacerbated by drinking.
As teenagers, my friend and I shoplifted
anything we could. Our universe's king barely cared.

But that king, I hear, killed himself.
Flipped his car purposely over a freeway median.
I hear when they cut open his freshly exited body

to determine if he was drunk or drugged or sick,
his belly was full of open cages. His throat,
filled with keys and hands. His head, I hear, a jar

of crushed plums. I'm left wondering who now
to rebel against. If she were alive, my friend
would tell me, *go home to your kids and don't look back.*

She'd say this but I would stay awhile to pet
the stray cat she'd feed. I would draw a line in the dirt.
I wonder if in my throat, my brain, there's not a key

or a cage, a hand or mottled pear, but a map, a kite,
a cigarette left for lighting. I tell my friend,
wherever she is, to run and never look back. I say

that people who grow up in sad houses
do not grow up to be happy. I say this also
to that dead king of stolen liquor and gum, my own

trauma and continuation on the examination table,
iced and imminent as plumes of nitrogen.
But it's no use. I have a cigarette and a map

of the city where I was born. Last sentences I will
exhale tonight: *We're all wondering*
what happened to each other. Reminiscence is an augury

backwards, a slow bullet returning to us, now.

SNAKES

The winter we all had the stomach flu. Kids irrational and curled on the floor.
Little doll fires. Then they would puke, heaving and retracting like novas.

I was sickest. Secretly pregnant, early along. My toddler, high on fever, met me
on the cold bath tile and closed my eyes. His hand left resting on my mouth.

I was the house's Earth, a shut-eyed, spinning matryoshka. Sun, reachable
and real—small, burning boy. His stink and breath. While gods closed,

opened doors on the star's surgical canopy (curved back or belly or thigh),
he found me somewhere new. His frustration and agony. Scratched my face

hard enough I bled. I slapped back. My son's stunned and quivering mouth.
I shouted: *don't touch me.* What I meant was: *I'm sorry you're sick. I will be*

your living braille. We calmed and stared off. Snakes shedding the mouse's weight.
Sleeping it away. All of it. Two weeks later, no longer pregnant and my secret

relief. Everyone forgave me. I dreamed that everyone forgave. I dreamed.

INK

The first time I watched something die, its eyes
opened at the last lived moment, death's first. A razor

between the two. The fledgling hawk's pupil turned so black
I felt as though I had been blindfolded and led high up

a cliff, then pushed. I didn't know dead eyes darken
or that watching them darken meant for the rest of my life

knowledge would carry with it a bottle of ink. Recently, everything
has been stained: stuffed toy bears, my daughter's fresh hair,

the dream in which I wear long white gloves I cannot remove,
while a wild pig plays like a dog with my children.

They are chasing each other, laughing. This pig
I'm about to skin grunts, the children grunt too. Strange voices

of the unconscious. But my gloves are too tight, and I wake
before killing. The lives and deaths of others are everywhere.

I once wrote a confession down but erased it. I once wore
a paper crown that caught fire, and when the burning

scent of hair filled the room, memory's open fume
evacuated my head to hover between mind and automation.

Afterwards, hair shorter, my mother putting away leftover
birthday cake, I wrote down a first truth: *I caught fire the day*

I turned twelve. My mother's arms and a blanket saved me.
Under them, blindness and weight. When ash hits water it floats

for a long time before becoming the whale's passenger,
and the whale before she swallows the ash is different

after she does. I wrote this today: *Our baby would have been*
born soon. His eyes would have been blue. To know this. It changes nothing.

BRIEF COLOR

The milk's spill reflects red next to the torn bear's heart.

While making dinner, I speak to my vanished brother. He announces

a black dog carrying in a gift of glistening pig bone

from a field filled with butterflies, filled with hunger.

Do you know the butterflies are scavengers? my brother asks.

I say, *I've seen a swallowtail enter an armadillo through its blown-out eye*

and emerge from the groin. My brother clicks his tongue, says, *the distance…*

The dog chews. The butterflies turn into candlelight against greasy plates

at night, while at my feet the hardwood floor reveals its rings

expanding out. I wonder if my brother ever used his pocketknife

to cut something loose so it became, while fleeing, a circle within a circle.

My two-year-old son drags his fingers through the milk,

and the puddle becomes a hurt wing. I wipe his hand clean.

He takes his torn bear close, kisses it. My brother asks,

Do you know never to be the cup?   *Yes,* I say. *I've watched water turn into air.*

Before he walks out the door, before air becomes a bell at my ankles,

my brother ends, *it will consume you.* Later, my daughter watches herself wet her face in the mirror. I lie in bed with her small, sleeping sibling.

He speaks nonsense in dream, but I hear it as question. I even bring to his eye

that brief color one cannot see when far, far away from home. I begin,

never be the boy who enters, exits this life. But I stop, start again, *never be the boy*

who will drop a stone…into the boat…into my chest.

THE CONQUEROR, 1956

*The filmmakers knew about the nuclear tests
but the federal government reassured residents
that the tests caused no hazard to public health.*

By the end of the movie, John Wayne's lungs
will have burned through his armor. The director's chair,

left out in the rain, will look as if

it has fever dreamed, and the director,
home by then in Los Angeles, will dream a heaviness

dropping from the sky. As it nears land,

he will wake to an idea regarding cause and effect:
the end does not stand still

but rises all around the place where it falls.

By the credits' last words, everyone
will have lost their breath.

A strand of blonde hair will have clung

to a stylist's discarded black smock,
and her black shadow, also discarded in Utah,

will grow so long and thin with trying to walk away

it snaps. From an army base in Kentucky,
my young father will watch this film skeptically.

After chowtime, the pursed mouth of Susan Hayworth

will whimper, *save me.* While my father drinks
in the celluloid-lit darkness

a cold glass of water, John Wayne

will become the golden face of ancient history. Later,
my father will stand rigid before his sergeant

and note the lines of the man's under-eyes.

He will think loyalty isn't really all that cinematic,
but rather, cracked, like a dishrag

left to harden over a fence. By the end

of the movie, my father will stare into a polished mirror,
flash to a photograph he once saw of the dead

and dying horses on the beach of Normandy just twelve years before.

(Sand fleas hopping on the horses' eyes.
Eyes that end when gazing at one, white sky.)

So many cast and crew members with terminal cancers

will drink from the same cold glass
as my young father. My father will outlive them,

though he might ask later, for what. (To understand better

the gun he talks to, or the bombs sleeping
inside their aluminum drums? To grow familiar with

the clouds and sound that fill the air, having gotten there

not from above, but from within?)
By the end of the movie, it will be the dirt

under the actors' nails that hums

well after their passing. When only my father and I are left
in a backyard in a small town where he's retired,

I'll think about the rain's angle, sip my wine, stay quiet.

In the conversation we'll never have,
I'll tell him not to look too long at whatever remains.

But he won't hear clearly, and will ask me to speak

again, louder this time. This time,
to pull a curtain over that bright cage.

This time, to make the horses go away.

BLACK ANTS

I believe them because their souls are figure eights.
I believe them when they say *the cornfield is sewn*
with vertigo. When I stare down the rows, I believe

the sky behind me makes promises
it outgrows. I believe it hurts to be shot.
I believe a gun aimed at the setting sun marks a scythe

in its blinding center. I believe that my father was once
a sharp thorn, and the snake he blew apart,
I believe its venom thickened inside a thin arm.

I believe that my father's boyhood snake-bitten friend
would have been a bad man had he survived.
I believe the story went, *before he got bit,*

Nick took a rock to a dog's head. I believed
my father, lucid and speaking gothic—
Nick was the kind of kid who hurt kittens and other kids.

I wanted to believe my father was never really
his friend, but my father reminded me
they grew up *in the middle of nothing. Sometimes bearing it*

is enough. And who is my father now that he no longer
remembers landscape. Or that he ever even told me
this story. I believe somewhere between the dead snake

and his dead friend, my father stands,
his back against the sun. I believe my father waits there
to tell me again what he's done, and the ants,

I believe their bodies lined up make bright rivers.
I've thrown a red apple against a house,
watched the juice-streaked window that I believed

was my kingdom pixelate black. The cracked glass
speaks back to me still: *Did you ever as a child watch a house
burn down? Did you ever as a child believe the boy*

who lit the match, the boy who ran, the boy who told you
to run towards the rivulet's end?

COEFFICIENT OF RESTITUTION

I talk quietly on the phone about something I don't want to do

but have to. (As a hand passes through dark, touch meets unseeable

surfaces: heavy wall, heavy bed, island, island, clearest glass empty

on the nightstand.) I whisper something abstract now: *We throw away*

what we love. I cannot see any future where this could—circumstance is instinct

and accident fallen into each other's orbits, the revolutions of which

I and whoever is on the other side of the phone collide against.

The sight of us from very far away also impacts this equation: the train

coming back from its vanishing point bridges or obliterates our entity.

To perceive this much when refusing that which I would do anything

to adore—I try, I try, or I go blind.

HURT MUSIC

The bell's emptied space
has no name. I would like

to call it my never-born.
I'm there and the metal clapper

and bowl are asleep.
My never-born is awake,

very quiet.

I don't want to reach
for him. I don't want to fall

from the rope's fray or draw
nothing from the naming. I call,

can you hear me? All parts
of the bell rouse differently.

The clapper,

in deepest dream, says,
breathe me back, breathe

me back. My matted lungs
search for air—the bowl

wakes dazed. *Hush now,*
it drones, *your hurt music.*

Dizzied

me, dark-circle-eyed in the curve's
continuum and orbit.

My unborn speaks
from inside his name, his last

wish reverberating:

Carry me in the bell, betrayer.
In the apogee of your voice

to my voice.

ROLL CALL (1)

I remember losing my face, young,
then looking for it years later, finding in the water
all the other drowned faces. I remember pulling from one

a pugilist's nose. Broken, reset. Arousal and apology.
I remember thinking that living contradicts itself.
That dying contradicts it too. I remember

blood and sneakers spread around my friend's head
in gym after he fell from the bleachers, his arms flailing
beyond the floor's sheen to come back paler. Later,

head pressed against a curtain of chrome and cosmos,
his eye's new-dark counting, counted. I remember
the number 3 tattooed across the drunk wrist

of my pseudo-grieving future-ex. Something about the father,
son, and Holy Ghost. About dedication to a dead
Irish grandfather. I remember visiting that country

with someone new and better, so much rain hung
on its saints, and the beach outside Dingle where we
kidnapped the community's dog for a day and renamed

him Bully. I remember drunk arguments. Broke, I said
I would sell all that I had just to stay. I remember believing
in detachment. A week later, even broker, I remember

calling my mother from a payphone, 21st century lip prints
and smut smudged across its plexiglass. I remember speaking
tersely and later, somewhere else, dreaming of oysters.

Digging, then their mute atria gasping in my pail. At my feet,
I remember looking down. I remember my face, too,
or some version of it, reflected in the shells. Taking from

their silver's wet my monoglot mouth, and from my mouth,
a hook. I remember my lip sewn to the air. And air, violent
and quiet, I remember it too, everywhere.

FAIRY TALE

At work on the playground, two brothers turn.
Two oiled and ready beasts against the rest—
a rock thrown to the heart of a boy all ribs

and eyes, another rock to the pink-lace face
of a girl, and me, a mortal dumb with sight,
drowning for a new moral. *To see is to be tainted.*

To follow is to fall. In another life, I was small
and lying beside a wolf. The sun couldn't measure
our wildness. In a moment it came to me:

if everything was new and anonymous, if sight
was genesis then God might define light itself
with this scene: my child-self as flame, the head

a torch, the wolf carrying me in his eye,
on his wet fang. But the life didn't end well.
Without warning it, I stabbed the wolf

in its yellow iris. Back at the playground,
another large rock thrown at my breast,
I whisper to one: *Jesus fucking Christ, kid,*

don't you know you can't hurt me? And he laughs
because he knows I'm wrong. If only I were
a better witch, able to turn sky into basement,

girl into surf, boy into tree, able to do anything
but envision myself someplace else where wolves
wear the skins of children, or, stuffed into the bellies

of wolves, terrible children wait for blood
to draw their fragile bodies again to the light.

AFTERLIVES

After I incised it, I offered up
to the bad wolf a vagary: pale kid,

(a window), living ghost to my edges.
Conjure only this much of being nine:

her lungs on ice. But sometimes it all comes back.
Memory, memory. My grandmother alive

and smoking. Her abusive,
loamed mouth and spectacle of hands

against broad white light on the porch.
As she gestures, swing singing high like knives

sharp and touching. Now I want
to lunge through the belly intercut

and for the wolf in this story to bleed the bed.
But instead, I will speak in zeros and without

looking back. The past is my proof of ends.
Every new encounter is with my own afterlives—

The soul bound by its eyeteeth
to private, necessary murders.

REBIRTH

When the feather appeared from my breast
I wouldn't name its color. I wouldn't
pluck it as if I would a word from a page
and allow it to disappear into memory.
When the beak broke my nose, I sang my old
language with a worm in it, and the worm dangled
with every exhale it took to conjure the distant
vowels of humanness. When the wings
made my ribs into a museum, people paid
to see. But I would not fly. Only answered
the people with a poem. The first or last line
was this: *because from eye, blossoms entrance...*
I don't remember the rest, except
there was you, perched on leaning stacks
of ruined books. I can't speak for much more
than wanting to pull a rock from the wreck,
to throw it at the closed window, so we
could both leave like seeds spit against the sky.

EVERYTHING CRUEL IS ALSO REAL

Starts a memory—you in a yellow dress against the condition

of your kite string. Taut, it lifts you with a thinnest white,

unwinding, tethered to you, kept like a conversation within your fists.

This could be the beginning or end of everything. Surely I must be dead,

watching with hollowed-out joy, your physics reaping the late lawn

of its light. I want to give you my hand in place of the wide sky—

the kite spread out against infinity, soundlessness telescoping

through distance. I'm afraid I'll never be as I once was. Later,

when ready to change from your yellow dress, I'll hear one,

extravagant scream. A wasp will fall from the sleeve, clean sting

in your armpit. I smash it with my hand as soon as it lands. You can't notice,

in your screaming, my coming back to life.

BURNING HAIR

This is my fortune: *its only obligation is to disappear.* I eat the paper

but not the shell. I light a tall candle and watch the flame.

A cheap vanilla scent in my food. I think of the desert in which

a version of me lived. A mountain lion that walked past

his wildness onto a neighbor's rock lawn. Somewhere inside me,

the slip of paper I might have misread. Maybe it said, *its only*

obligation is to eat. Preyed upon, I once pressed my small paws

against the lion's jaws and waited for a human word to come

from my mouth. In one year, I will not live in this rented house.

When the vase breaks against the driveway the shards will reflect the blue

scattered eye that sees clearly when one thing shatters into many.

By the tall candle tonight, I'm aroused by the smell of my hair,

burning now, one plucked strand at a time. I light up, extinguish,

over and over. In one hundred years, none of us will be alive.

Each of us the spinning silver of a childhood pinwheel,

the blood on a tongue after losing a milk tooth. The instinct to chew

even as our breath against red gives names to the animals we eat.

STRANGE HANDS

This morning, my son dug a hole—buried his toy car, outgrown shoe,

a spoon. In one year, new tenants will find the shoe surfaced

from mud, call it ghostly, throw it away. The heavy rain will smell of dirt

absolving a worm, fresh and wet, and in strange hands

the artifacts of my son that he won't see again until they come back

as horse, bucket, cloud. In the new city in which I'll live, where rain

will smell the same, I'll urge a worm back into the ground. The shoe, too,

its laces taking patient root. Disappearance not as ghost, not as bone,

but as the boy's first knowledge of return.

ELLIPSIS

*The drowned boy was 3-year-old Aylan Kurdi,
from Syria, part of a group of 23 trying
to reach the Greek island of Kos.*

In a lit, almost drained pool at night,
I once saw a snake swimming back and forth,

back and forth. He slid his head

up and against the yellow cement wall
to smell with his tongue the distance out.

His shadow was the only familiar word

from an otherwise estranged body.
We must stay calm, I told him, though

he was trapped and I was walking

away. Between fidelity and rescue,
the make-believe limitations of choice.

For the rest of my life, I will tack

the image of the snake to a boat
rowed slowly. The boy I'll never know

will dip his oar into the ocean,

recite his best wish, over
and over. Back and forth.

Trying to think of a next, selfish line,

I'll hear his breath like white noise.
(*Looking past the water's surface, pennies*

in blue sleep. Is it not built into our eyes

to be sorry?) But then, I will decide
to listen, much too late to adore

the boy. Whatever's left of him

will kiss an obscure shore—as if
the boy could ask: *do we not all have*

some place more human to go?

INDEXICAL

This book I open is meant to remind me
of what happened in the past.

The time I drew a line in a dark bar

and slid an ice cube across the wood.
We burned ourselves up to get where we couldn't

have been. To confront my opacity, I pressed

a candle against my palm. October leaves
assemble a necessary message, the bright red

of their dying a symptom of denial.

The weather knows there is no such thing
as the absolute absence of hope. I doubt

in a year we will even be talking.

The invisible wire stretching from your finger
to my chest will spit electricity,

but no one will be left to seal it. This is when

the relationship between my eye
and the empty room will indicate you are gone,

if you were ever there, whoever you are,

and whatever it does to want for us,
in our nothingness, the condition

under which we come back.

IN MEDIAS RES

I once imagined my life differently,
but no one hears, so I say it again, and again,

until the words turn to ice, clear and contained

as the actress on stage who seems
to have forgotten her line, seems to have just realized

the face she wants most to wear

is that of warmed brass, of west, of a door
undressed, whatever comes with entering

the reckoning scene, the one in which nothing happens

except our living children streaking shirtless
across the lens, young as they are

but will not always be, while across the street

a neighbor watches somebody else water
white flowers until the whole lawn looks jeweled,

and, fresh with exhumation, an unnegotiable grub

readies in the beak of a bird.

PERIGEE

"All I remember is a gush of wind, and then the sound. Leo, who was standing next to me, wasn't standing next to me. He was off to the side."

—a witness reporting what he remembers after
Adacia Chambers crashed her car into a crowd
of people at Oklahoma State University's Home-
coming Parade, killing four and injuring forty-four.

Do you know that people died? As a child, I believed
a floating pinpoint of dust was so relative I cried

and kicked when it faded. Close as possible, my eye

must have seemed like a blinking satellite reentering at night
to the mote's microscopic lives.

Do you understand what you've done? Her answer is not

a house but its doors. (The distance between
beginning and end is a formless, unpredictable matter.)

Do you understand what has happened? Her chest fills

with baths burning to white. A family dog sleeps
through the day, and the moon in a hungry haze opens

the fridge for some milk. The moon, the dog,

and the family who won't come home tonight
huddle closer and closer in an aperture like exit wound.

Do you understand you hurt a lot of people? Her hand

is a bandaged bomb. A burst fist gripped by little dolls,
stuffed bears in chairs, the mutt in his rescuing kingdom.

Do you understand why you're here? Her answer is not

a room but its walls blown down, the airborne rubble
elided with light and twinkling as though America

from space. If I move close enough now to the lit image

of my country in that arrested moment of orbit,
I see only the beginning and ending.

Do you understand what you've done? Her answer is not

a place but its entity trying to find a word for time
when dropped as though ink into its own inevitable proximity.

NOSTALGIA FOR THE ABSOLUTE

The crow nests in a tree with a plaque, the place
a football player in summer training got struck

by lightning and died. It was the 1960s

and all the young girls who loved him
and all the mothers and fathers planted the tree

where he fell. There's nothing special about his name,

William. It makes me think of any football field,
the girls whose toes get muddy from the steps taken up,

down the bleachers. Their blonde hair straight

like church windows that flood then burn with light.
Those blue eyes turn up when asked anything.

Like, *no way* to that "death-tree" which resembles

the silhouette of the weird girl, an ecology taking shape
as she poses on the turf, equating the blackness

of night to a shade of burial. That's like my friend Therese,

who, bored one night, drove her car to the edge
of a lake and got shot and killed by a stranger.

I suppose there's nothing special about her name either,

though in Greek she is *Reaper*. If I think of her now
she's reappearing from beneath the bleachers, a halo

of gun smoke rising from her black T-shirt's center.

Another *O* coming from her mouth. Darkest bowl
of stars yet, even when mapped with something bronze

and engraved. This easiest tactic of heartbreak, as if to tame,

not hurt, the worm that grows inside. To show the crows
that the coins can be plucked after all from our friends' eyes

and dropped like yesterday's leaves where we forget to ever look.

A SCENE

When told decay
has made its way into his absolute,

where thinnest vessels flicker

in synapse and in remembered birdsong, he wants,
as if to overflow

with a stranger's skin, to be a starfish,

headless, brainless, with no horizon left
by his evolution: weapon to himself, weaponless.

And when the doctor delivers the prognosis,

every word now a war between rust and water,
the man doesn't recognize all those losses

parading the bone-white god's breath

of x-ray with its careful promises,
because the man, now a starfish, cannot care less

about a god's existence.

AFTER THE STROKE

Carried through the night by helicopter,
surrounded by floating paramedics,
you stiffened against your strange air bed,
one you would have called merciless
had you not been flying your way to a distant
Houston hospital,

preparing for a president's landing,
the air sharply cold on your white sheets,
your stately quiet and brain
like an aquarium for all the forms of life
you could no longer remember.

~

When I was your child asleep,
you told me:

shark teeth might glint in the dark,
but that shark will guard you
even as you reach and rise for air;

it's an animal's only work to bear it.

~

A shark guarded you that night,
circling your own abrupt dream,
until the water there cycloned,
your own childhood lifting up
before you like a kite.

Now, it is my turn to assure you:

God is no man after all, no woman,
but a small, dark-haired boy
reflected in the water. He is you,
cutting the kite strings
that tangle and disturb

the gray Gulf of Mexico, where
the shark's pinhole eyes will not dim
until you've come back to kick
the sand, the sky, the ocean's will
and wind.

HOPING WHEREVER YOU ARE, YOU ARE NOT WATCHING

Our father cannot sleep. Tomorrow, he will kill your dogs

because they killed his cat. Our father will lose his mind, briefly.

He will shoot your dogs in the woods at the edge of town,

so his neighbors don't hear the rasp of the dogs' bodies

against leaves shed bomb-like from white. Then, no one but our father

will witness the dirt spilling a testimony of ants and worms

so the ground becomes one with everything. In this trial of willing

you and your dogs to the widening, altered sky, I will call,

but you will not answer, because you, like our father, cannot,

could not ever, bear the asking noise of my voice.

REMAINDER

After you asked me to leave
I went to my room and listened to the radio's static.

In its storming, my ears turned to mud.
When I lay my head on the floor,

I left a stain as round and dark as a hole.
When I reached in, my fingers touched

the hard doors of your eyes. They were wet,
as if your face had broken open.

My hand then: a rock, a weapon.

~

Where I live now, a bell tower
divides sunlight on a lawn

where coal dust once tangled people
to sepia and twigs. Just beyond the tower,

a coal stack opens its one, deep eye.

~

I believe
when you put a gun to your throat

you too were gazing up,
leaning your eyes heavenward

to a cumulonimbus gap
where the weight of falling rain

became your only care.

Clouds might have gathered on your chest
until you were heavy with fog.

No one knew you had gone to the woods
without a map.

You didn't leave behind a letter
explaining yourself. Your residue,

like the coal stack's, greasing
ghosts you couldn't name

or even speak about.

And man,
I hear you were wearing yourself badly

the days before you disappeared.
I'd seen it before: your eyes

distinct with vanishing, absent
as shadows curling

your face to smoke.

~

I wonder if you, somewhere in the woods,
thought of me, clean and resilient.

Where I live now,
the trees, upset some nights, collide with themselves

through darkness.

Some nights,
I think of you this way:

colliding with trees
to return from wherever you've been,

quiet as ever,
having sewn into your throat a diamond so big

you can't swallow.

POEM FOR INFINITE RETURNS

—for R.D. (1935–2011)

This is when the sun is more
than just the sun, but I cannot
give it a better name, and you,

whoever you will become, will relearn
the sun as brighter than a penny.
A penny, that if tasted, tastes like blood

and the beginning of blood. *R,*
this is me speaking to you:
A poem where your chair will bare

its bones to an empty house.
Mellowed light will stain
the curtains gold. Weightless,

and unhurting now, your hands
won't disturb the window's lace
to show the neighborhood your new

and vanished self, standing, not standing,
as you hover moth-like
on your ghost's difficult net.

And wherever you are now,
I'd like to know the color of the sky,
because I will not see it here.

I will not make a metaphor of you either.
Instead, in this poem, you are yourself,
waving goodbye on your way

to the Cumberland River,
pulling your boat behind your car
like a boy and his roan horse

off to split the warm wind
with their teeth and chests, wet and white
below the sun's burst fist.

DECEMBER LIGHT IN ARIZONA

We were in the cemetery again,
a fever rising in us like some bright
horizon. The headstone names around us
fooled you into thinking we weren't so
dangerously alone, filling ourselves
with red wine and the cruel, heavy sound
of truck horns. I said the highway looked
like bone, an arm outstretched
forever across the dust. Our eyes burned
from looking. The dark nooks of our ears filled
with birdsong, then silence, then, remember?
You fell into one of those empty graves
and almost broke, with your perfect body,
the sky's horrendous, vacant mirror.

ROMANCE AT THE ABANDONED MINE

Dear X,

You and I divide in secret
like zygotes. Outside my window,
forsythias beg to catch a fledgling's drop.
Their yellow buds poke the air with hurt,
and God exits their faces
with hurt sighs.

X,

Sometimes, even God wants to say yes
before he says no.

Darling X,

I remember it this way:
Light hardened
to bone and spread our bodies
across the landscape. Pines
and ghosts welcomed us
to their winter's stage. Even the air
smoked, unfiltered. Black
calcified branches seduced
into crossing the sky's cold.
Every tree there, giant-tall,
gazed through us

where we walked as invisibles
down the stone altars and ruinous stairs.

Oh X,

I would have taken my clothes off then
if you had asked me to. I would
have done almost anything for you.

And for the place, maybe, itself.
I would have even said yes
to being a ghost
if it had meant staying there, if it had meant
walking through walls
of light, rigid with desire and haunting's
old pleasure: to outlive a moment

by not leaving it.

PARADOX

The heart
cannot be chewed down to wish.
It cannot talk to the ribs or pelvis—
those rock cradles
bound by their hard and honest suit
of machine.

The heart cannot speak at all without
metaphor; imagination is rumor
and breath colliding in its dark
avenues, seducing the meat from
its born muteness. The heart is more
than red and pulse, more, even,
than a cell's want for soul.

So when

the heart takes a name and greets me
on the outside or calls me on the telephone,
I realize I'm not dead yet,
that I can come back from fading
into the body's old routine
of being alive:

that animal etiquette
when the heart is just a lonely muscle,
and language,

just a tongue not knowing, not even touching,
another tongue.

ADAM IN LOVE

Time leads us always—whither—we do not wish to go.
To Love Time.

—Simone Weil

The apple smokes on its branch, or pretends to.
Because it doesn't want to fall, it makes itself

sexy for the tree. Or is it this place, or the light

that is sexed, and the apple, just a thing after all.
The thing, foreplay in its first container,

just pretty enough for wanting—but the sparrow

is content with the worm, the worm content
with its short life. Adam, in love, is happy

just to watch the burning horizon of Eve's jaw, to feel

his hunger as living's gift. Yet the apple still wears
its wet, teasing faces. To see is almost to know:

juice, throat, worm, bird, and, *oh*, the human thigh,

removing its damp towel to come at last into focus.
Even the light is erotic. Even that tangled tree.

Adam thinks he would like to fuck the fruit.

But the unarousable worm splits into two, a head,
a crotch for each. This is when the Vaseline

is wiped from the lens, brothers and sisters. When we

become so good at desire, we achieve
beginning and end all at once. Climax and ruin.

That poor, patient Adam who knows too much now,

whispers in his extinct tongue: *I do not love time, I love time,*
I do not love. The risk of remembering is guilt, my friends,

and the clock's beating lockstep, real.

MERCY

You spoke nonsense in your fever: *my mother*

would hate me for this. You smoked cigarettes in a backless

gown and waved traffic on, hopeful a hit-and-run would tear

from your young body the catheter that drew from you

a cloud pink with poisoned blood. In your medicated confusion,

another patient stared at the horizon of your forehead

and crossed herself. Her saints were not your saints. If your

mother had known, I think she would have joined hands

with that woman and prayed right there on the sidewalk,

loving you through your cursing and delirium. But no one

had called to tell her that, in another hour, your arm would

be amputated in a room adorned with wide, Modigliani eyes.

And when you told the doctors you didn't think that would

be necessary, the eyes closed and imagined a time when people

were given sainthood, back when the line from your finger

to your heart might have led straight to God.

HALF-LIFE

—for J.O. (1975-2010)

I don't know if I ever saw you
from the store window, walking down
your staircase, driving to work, coming home again.
If I had to guess, I did.

If a tree you know well falls in the night, it's like a horse
with his head and neck down, drinking from a bucket,
his tongue dipped in meditation, not about to give over
to a fly, the sound of its wings

spread in the air, two bodies glued to themselves
while the rest of the world sleeps in the dark rooms that erase
the episode of the horse drinking,
allowing the fly to devour him.

~

That was in the details of your nightmare:
the stray dog you might have loved, eating deeply
from your hand, was suddenly hit by a car
and spun into the early sky like a pocketful

of ruddy coins. It's hard to say
why the dream was even there,
or how it became like a worm
that grew, inside you, from almost nothing.

~

I went to the deli next to your house today.
The crepe myrtles are blooming. Nothing has changed.
Your house is the same. The women and children
are still beautiful. But I admit

I find you in the details:

the mosaic facing east looks like you,
its folding and unfolding
hands reminiscent of flame,
where the boy with burned skin and cracked lips

reaches into the river's dark loam, retrieves
a glass bottle, a bottle cap, a pocket watch,
and a hook. But of course,
you are not made from treasures, or anything

but abandoned air.

~

You were the thin, redheaded boy
who wouldn't expose your chest for fear
it would make you virginal in the eyes of everyone.
You were the boy sliding your hand into the river,

soaking your shirt cuff for the walk home. No one knew
you could be so nonchalant. One day you stripped naked
and sunburned so badly your skin peeled away as if
your body was spread over

with maple leaves.

~

You had the final say, whoever you were.
You, uncounting a row of cars until the parking lot
was an open cage, the familiar things of a neighborhood
gone through its door—

a stray dog crossed the street to follow a bird
into the sky. The bird, you thought, was an idle witness
to a newest absence. And maybe you were consoling
the neighborhood,

its cancer of windows flush against lace.
But I won't talk anymore
of your delusions
the morning you killed yourself,

when you got out of bed,

unspoke your first words,
unwrapped yourself for the blackened bardo.

You must have been the bare-chested boy again.

Thin, easy as ash,
shedding his first and last fires.

FREAK

Open his mouth for a word and it will be *tooth*. As in, he'll pull

a tooth from a previous life and bring back with it

his first, faraway curse. He'll conjure the hush that began sometime

around birth. He'll pull his cradle's ribs down from the bough

and lacquer them in gravity. Notice in the new sheen

of this glazed eve that there is language even in silence.

He'll move closer to the page and reveal he's part tongue, part tree.

The hounds had him too young. The eucalyptus that raised him

dropped its branches in the fertile winds. On the playground

they called him freak. Said his eyes were bearded orchids, his thousand

thin and flickering arms were snakes. If he could go back now,

he'd untangle from his hair a crown of canaries. He'd set them free

against the bullies' eyes, bellies, and chests. (Canaries aren't always meant

to return. Some lives begin and end in levitation.) As always,

he would say nothing. Or, nothing but *yellow*. As in, he'd pull

the yellow light from a previous life and bring back with it

the ground's deep and sparkling strange ones.

EYETEETH

At night, the kitchen's reminiscent of a late wife,

her vodka bottle and a potato's five eyes wallow in a cruel joke

of origin. The vodka dreams its Russian mother, the potato

also dreams its Russian mother. A crisis of privacy leads me here.

Last night's dinner plate: grease, habit. My face: oxygen, document.

I listen to Leonard Cohen and drink small consolations.

This song portrays Janis Joplin giving him *head on the unmade bed*

while the limousines wait in the street. Beyond my pantry and cans,

there must be a limousine. Suddenly, I miss my ex. The one I used

to call a weed. My urgency. To write down all the things I believe

are real: ice in the glass, a blow job, the cut avocado I eat every

morning, my old dog tasting on the stench of her fur a previous life.

This irritating click and suck of consciousness. So often I ask my house

for its honesty. It answers back: stacking doll, rind, bitch,

chanteuse, fist. I ask again. This time, what is memory made of?

The house answers: compass, compulsion, headlights fugitive at night,

teeth speaking their white, a birthday cake on fire, a mirror's

ten thousand scraped and silver darlings.

BIRD OF PARADISE

When the bogeyman
came to me recently,
his face and claws cloaked,
I confess I bent. I told him

everything. I pulled his gloves
off his terrible, dripping hands
and kissed them like I would a king's.
He was my lilac,

and even his steps
rang out like a lilac's wet,
velvet sleep.

~

I visited graves today.
It took so long to find yours
I thought I'd imagined your passing.
By the time I saw the headstone,

I had believed you back to me
and attached my grief to some unknowns:
a family of six in a green row,
fossilized in death's most intimate clichés—

loving mother and *father, loving sons* and *daughters.*

~

As a child, I stepped off the bed
into a lake. You waded in,
sateen swan
coming toward the dream's

hot paradise. Sleep blackened,
my eye's rapidity
collected these poses
for the moon's sunken waking.

~

I remember the house I grew up in
filled with objects and fire.
You and I dine there around a vase. I think
the flowers are birds of paradise, lonely exotics

that look to be burning in their middles, bright
rivulets I can still see in night's climax.
The bogeyman comes toward us there.
Apologetic and winded, he sits, unfolds his napkin.

We welcome him, he who is in need of kindness.
And anyway, how could you have known
or even widened
your mouth's muted o?

While the child I once was watched from her chair
as you turned to bird or statuary. Stiff in delusion,
your new tongue fumbled the air
I forgot was there until it wasn't.

AS BEGINNING, AS END

When my daughter says she wants her infancy back
I say I would go back too, when I could still hold her,

when I could speak saturnine and aloud, like this:
Someday I will vanish inside you. You will

think of me like ocean in a shell. And then, too,
my tired nonsense: *You're a bird. You're a bird.*

Always, my daughter wouldn't answer but stare
with her wet, infant eyes like teacups on a burning

blanket. I would continue, sometimes, like this:
there's a cliff leaving its height inside me.

Now in the future where my daughter, so close to grown,
says: *I want to be yours again, to root,*

to nurse. I realize it is she who has disappeared.
That first version of herself, all tangle

before word, tears to show her hunger, no question yet,
no answer even expected. I speak in my way:

We have left each other
for each other. The body wishes. The body is a wish.

ROLL CALL (2)

I used to think
the remembered shape of an animal
sank into my own. Older now

my thoughts turn to the prized bones within
their careful, white devotions.
I remember sex in a car. The look

my thigh took in dark. A ghost loin.
I remember the stars like critics.
Watching, distant, unarousable.

I remember that boy I loved
scraping away the silver of a mirror,
coming toward me with a dog

he had found on the street.
We named her after the science of surprise.
Later, the name became the small

broken marriage of my teens,
gymnasium carnations burning
our wrists down to desire. My adolescent

half-life like a cheap, lingering odor.
I remember my very first dog
handed to me after its bottle-feeding.

Taken early from her mother,
my father told me she might not make it
through the night.

But the dog grew as big as me.
If I look now I see her white chest
and my first boyfriend's hand

like a doorway to the hour, and my father,
who is fading also, in the details:
his ear against a rib, slowed pounding

of the inside places. Veins, throat, thought.

WEST

My husband and I are chasing the eclipse, and our children,

strapped in the backseat, are fighting, so I daydream

that bridge bats rupture from beneath an overpass, shrill shapes

without course. I've been on trips like this before,

but this time I am dead, I died a year ago, and it's only my afterimage

positioned in the passenger seat. I'm told the light around us

will turn platinum when the sun goes black. I'm told, given

my condition, my children will charge straight through my chest as if

about to take flight, my hands, atmosphere that they are, will cool

for those two-and-a-half minutes of solar rarity. But for now,

passing one of those enormous, white wind turbines, I wish

I could witness it being put together, could see the assembling machines

as they raise and lock the blades onto its indisputable torso.

I could ask my husband, who knows that I am love with someone else,

why, in life, I never held the long rope that leads to the center

of the engine or heart or whatever one calls the massive, hovering power

that extends its arms above our American horizon. *Because,* he would answer, *you were and will always be a soul afraid of change.*

I'd mutter back: *We were supposed to go east, but the meteorologists predicted*

weather. (And if change is possible then it comes with looking through

the compass needle's eye, careful not to puncture one's cheek.)

I'd even try to explain this in the few ways left to me: *My life, our life*

together, depended so much on roadside omens. We'll watch this eclipse

from an abandoned school yard. Then, to prepare the air for my useless

caution: *our eager children will be the ones who break the gates open.*

GREEN

We will not die young from heart attacks.
The reasonable trees see this much

from their heights. I watch ambulances

pass by and wonder who's inside.
I've never before felt so convinced

by my skin's vast facts,

or by the wet of my blood hiding within
whatever this is that I am. Your arm

extended from the shower, your body

an avenue to your curtained body, living collects
in steam, but then, time runs out,

and I'm driving away on a hard highway.

I'm not ready, I say, *I do not want to go.*
The car carves my loneliness through

indivisible air. Ambulances passing me by—

the knowledge that death is unknowable.
Private, until it isn't. (Our initials

in clean wood.) Memory gets off

to the sound of a voice, to an image
defined by its extinction. One absence taking

custody of another until the grass's sudden green

pokes through the machine, until the clear
window intersects

your face. Your face, a moment

that I continue to leave, I find again in the days
of indifference that I act most like a cold key,

locking and unlocking. I'll tell you also

that I glimpse, from this highway,
a slender dead cow off to the asphalt side,

not at all gruesome, back turned to fast traffic.

Haunches and spine, black and intact.
I want to know more about her—

slow beast, consumed but never looked to,

and who, from a greater height,
might have seemed to live a decent life

until some urge spoke *go*, and walked her

past the fence's broken wire.
Because sometimes the boundaries

we encounter are not real. From our first

bench in the light, I want to talk
to you again, something as direct

as an upside-down cup:

when you and I drive away, what
will we observe from our wide window?

Once again, only in memory, your arm

extends from the shower. Our anxieties
over death, over divorce and children,

stare out like fallen fruits. I pick up

a piece to give the brief fly a name.
I hold the rotten pear

and tell the leaves above me that I've come here

to watch them change.

NOTES

This book's epigraph is borrowed from the 2010 Joanna Newsom song "Baby Birch" from the album *Have One on Me*.

The note starting "*The Conqueror*, 1956" is from *The Conqueror* (film) Wikipedia page.

The poem "Perigee" was written during my brief time in Stillwater, OK, as a PhD candidate in 2015. A woman, Adacia Chambers, crashed her car into the homecoming parade, killing four. I read witness Mark McNitt's quote on CNN.com. (The Leo of his quote and my son Leo bear no relation to one another.)

The poem title "Nostalgia for the Absolute" is borrowed from George Steiner's 1974 collection of CBC Massey lectures.

The epigraph to "Adam in Love" is from *The Notebooks of Simone Weil*, published first (in French) in 1956.

The poem "Eyeteeth" references Leonard Cohen's song "Chelsea Hotel #2."

ACKNOWLEDGMENTS

Acknowledgment is due to the following publications in which these poems, in some stage or form, originally appeared:

2013 Tupelo Press 30/30 Anthology, 2015 Best of the Net Anthology, The Adroit Journal, Bat City Review, The Collagist, Crab Orchard Review, DIAGRAM, Four Way Review, Linebreak, The Monarch Review, Mead, Mid-American Review, Ninth Letter, PHANTOM, Rockhurst Review, Superstition Review, Tongue, TriQuarterly, Tupelo Quarterly, and *Winter Tangerine*

Some of the poems in this manuscript appear in my chapbook *Futures with Your Ghost* (Finishing Line Press, 2014).

Thank you to Elizabeth Spires for selecting my poem, "Everything Cruel Is Also Real" (originally "A Vision"), for an Academy of American Poets Prize, and to Matthew Olzmann and Gabriel Blackwell at *The Collagist*, as well as John Wang at *Juked*, for nominating my work for Pushcart Prizes. Thank you, also, to John James and the editors at *PHANTOM* for a Best of the Net nomination. My deepest gratitude to Bruce Bond for selecting "Poem for Infinite Returns" for inclusion in the 2015 Best of the Net Anthology, as well as his generous words regarding this manuscript. Tarfia Faizullah, a poet I admire so much, thank you for your words and support, as well.

This book wouldn't exist without the consideration, instruction, guidance, and crystal-clear insight of my teachers: Norman Dubie, Jeannine Savard, Kate Daniels, Rick Hilles, Mark Jarman, Claudia Emerson, Joanie Mackowski, and Lisa Lewis.

Deepest gratitude to Christine Stroud at Autumn House for her hard work and care and to Alberto Ríos for choosing this book from many wonderful manuscripts.

Thank you to these inspiring writers and readers, as well: Amanda Abel, Aaron Alford, Elizabeth Barnett, Rebecca Bernard, Chris Burawa, Whitney Campbell, Lee Conell, Kendra DeColo, Cara Dees, Josh Jennings, Claire Jordan, Liz Lampman, Daniel Lebret, Ben Lesousky, Trey Moody (for believing in this book so much that you read it one hundred and one times), Andrew Rahal, Erin and Tomas Radcliffe, and Liz Solomon.

My children, Wren and Leo, thank you for being our bright continuum. Thank you, Chris, for being their wonderful dad.

And to the Oracle, I hear it all, clearly.

MELISSA CUNDIEFF received an MFA in poetry from Vanderbilt University, where she was the recipient of an Academy of American Poets Prize. Her poems appear in places such as *Best of the Net*, *Crab Orchard Review*, *Ninth Letter*, *Four Way Review*, *TriQuarterly*, *The Adroit Journal*, and *Tongue*. Originally from Texas, she lives in St. Paul, MN.

2017 & 2018 RELEASES

Apocalypse Mix by Jane Satterfield
WINNER OF THE 2016 AUTUMN HOUSE POETRY PRIZE
Selected by David St. John

Heavy Metal by Andrew Bourelle
WINNER OF THE 2016 AUTUMN HOUSE FICTION PRIZE
Selected by William Lychack

RUN SCREAM UNBURY SAVE by Katherine McCord
WINNER OF THE 2016 AUTUMN HOUSE NONFICTION PRIZE
Selected by Michael Martone

The Moon is Almost Full by Chana Bloch

Vixen by Cherene Sherrard

The Drowning Boy's Guide to Water by Cameron Barnett
WINNER OF THE 2017 RISING WRITER PRIZE
Selected by Ada Limón

The Small Door of Your Death by Sheryl St. Germain

Darling Nova by Melissa Cundieff
WINNER OF THE 2017 AUTUMN HOUSE POETRY PRIZE
Selected by Alberto Ríos

Carry You by Glori Simmons
WINNER OF THE 2017 AUTUMN HOUSE FICTION PRIZE
Selected by Amina Gautier

Paper Sons by Dickson Lam
WINNER OF THE 2017 AUTUMN HOUSE NONFICTION PRIZE
Selected by Alison Hawthorne Deming

FOR OUR FULL CATALOG PLEASE VISIT: HTTP://WWW.AUTUMNHOUSE.ORG